P9-BZI-089

2/05

ROCK & ROLL
HALL OF FAMERS

The Beatles

JIM WENTZEL

the rosen publishing group's
rosen
central

To Amy and Hugo, With All My Loving

Published in 2002 by The Rosen Publishing Group, Inc.
29 East 21st Street, New York, NY 10010

Copyright © 2002 by The Rosen Publishing Group, Inc.

First Edition

Library of Congress Cataloging-in-Publication Data

Wentzel, Jim, 1968–
The Beatles / by Jim Wentzel.— 1st ed.
p. cm. — (Rock & roll hall of famers)
Includes discography, filmography, list of Web sites,
bibliographical references, and index.
ISBN 0-8239-3526-4 (library binding)
1. Beatles—Juvenile literature. 2. Rock musicians—England—
Biography—Juvenile literature. [1.Beatles. 2. Musicians. 3. Rock
music.] I. Title. II. Series.
ML3930.B39 W45 2002
782.42166'092'2—dc21

2001004137

Manufactured in the United States of America

CONTENTS

The Beatles were perhaps the most popular and talented rock and roll group of all time.

Introduction

If you turned on an American television set in the summer of 1957, you might have spotted President Dwight D. Eisenhower addressing the nation, or Willie Mays shagging fly balls in center field for the New York Giants. You'd notice that automobiles had tailfins, and that

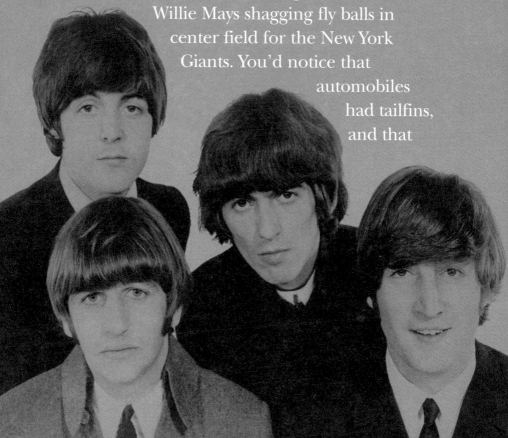

The Beatles

As teenagers, the Beatles were influenced by rockers like Elvis Presley.

gasoline was advertised at forty-five cents a gallon. You also might have caught a young rock and roller named Jerry Lee Lewis pounding a piano while belting out "Whole Lotta Shakin' Going On." If you happened to be a teenager in Liverpool, England, in 1957, and were interested in pop music, you might have heard some of the rock music coming from America—you would definitely have heard of Elvis Presley, at the very least. By that time, Elvis, his music, and his youthful swagger had crossed the ocean and started to influence teenagers all over the world in many ways.

In the midst of these events, in July of 1957, sixteen-year-old John Lennon was introduced to fifteen-year-old Paul McCartney at a church fair in Liverpool where John was performing with his group, the Quarry Men. Both John and Paul had modest musical backgrounds at a young age: Paul had taught himself some guitar and John led his own group. Both wrote songs even then, but neither could have dreamed where a simple talent for songwriting would eventually take them.

It is hard to imagine what the world would be like today if this meeting had never occurred. From this simple introduction sprang a friendship that would last until 1970, when they would decide to end their partnership. In the years between 1960 and 1970, John and Paul were the leaders of a pop music phenomenon known as the Beatles. The Beatles wrote and performed songs that not only became huge, popular hits, but also touched people's lives in the process. And not just a few people—millions and millions of people. For a time in 1964, the Beatles had the top five hit singles in the *Billboard* pop chart, a feat that no one would have thought possible and that still has not been equaled.

Beatlemania, the hysterical fan worship of the Beatles, started in England but spread worldwide.

With the hits, and the fame that came with it, also came influence. The Beatles' presence is still felt in the way music is made today; while making their records, they invented dozens of the techniques that have become standard in music recording studios. They changed the clothes people wore and the length of their hair. And most of all, they changed the world's attitude toward what the younger generation could do. Their rise to superstardom seemed to happen at precisely the right time, as if the world had been waiting just for them. Seeing thousands of screaming teenagers greeting them in the street wherever they went must have struck many as simple mass hysteria that would soon fade away with the next fad. But their legacy is still very much alive today.

In many ways, the Beatles are almost as popular today as they were over thirty years ago. In 1995, ABC aired *The Beatles Anthology,* a lengthy documentary about the group, narrated entirely by the Beatles themselves. This attracted millions of viewers and reminded many of just how powerful their impact had been, and still remains. A recent album of all of their number one hits—called simply *1*—has sold millions of copies and introduced the group to a younger generation. You can travel the world and still hear their songs coming out of radios everywhere, every day.

"The Beatles somehow reached more people, more nationalities, more parts that other bands couldn't reach," said Beatles guitarist George Harrison. "I think we gave hope to the Beatle fans." Although many reasons for their longevity and importance have been suggested, the Beatles' significance to the world can probably be summed up with one quality: They were the very best at what they did.

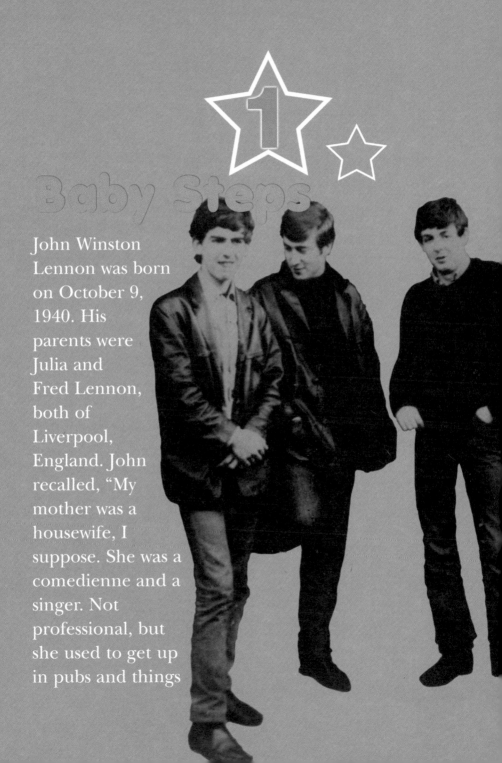

Baby Steps

John Winston
Lennon was born
on October 9,
1940. His
parents were
Julia and
Fred Lennon,
both of
Liverpool,
England. John
recalled, "My
mother was a
housewife, I
suppose. She was a
comedienne and a
singer. Not
professional, but
she used to get up
in pubs and things

like that. She had a good voice." Julia's sister Mimi primarily raised John from the time he was eighteen months old. As a young child, John showed little interest in music or music lessons, though at the age of ten he taught himself to play basic songs on the harmonica. "At sixteen, my mother taught me music," he explained. "She first taught me how to play banjo chords—that's why in very early photos of the group [the Quarry Men] I'm playing funny chords—and from that I progressed to guitar."

In 1956, the appearance of Elvis Presley's "Heartbreak Hotel" on the top of the charts in fourteen different countries (including England) marked a pop music milestone, and had a huge impact on John. "Nothing really affected me until Elvis," he explained. "Rock 'n' roll was real, everything else was unreal," he added. "It was the only thing to get through to me out of all the things that were happening when I was fifteen."

James Paul McCartney was born in Liverpool on June 18, 1942, to Mary and Jim McCartney. Paul's father had been a bandleader in Liverpool in the early 1920s, and was the only Beatle parent with any experience as a musician. Like John, Paul showed little interest in music as a child. At one point, he did make an effort to learn the piano (his father had once told him, "Learn the piano, because you'll get invited to parties"), but didn't like the fact that he had to apply himself to it. When Paul was fourteen, his father bought him a cheap guitar after Paul started listening to American rock and roll on the radio and was inspired to make music of his own. Among the first songs he learned to play were Elvis songs. "Any time I felt low I just put on an Elvis song and I'd feel great, beautiful," he said. Paul has never had true formal musical training, something which he is almost proud of now. "To this day, I have never learnt to write or read music," he said. "I have a vague suspicion that it would change how I'd do things."

The Meeting

John and Paul both grew up entirely in Liverpool, attending different schools but sharing similar passions, unbeknownst to each other. It wasn't

A fifteen-year-old John Lennon performs with his skiffle group, the Quarry Men.

until a church fair in July 1957 that they actually met, introduced by a mutual friend who thought they'd hit it off. John had formed a skiffle group called the Quarry Men in early 1957. Skiffle was a kind of homemade music based on rock and roll rhythms that was played on instruments like guitars and washboards, and had become wildly popular in England around that time. John was the singer and the natural leader, being confident and the most enthusiastic about the music.

On meeting Paul at the church fair, John was impressed at Paul's ability to tune a guitar. Paul also knew all the words to rock and roll tunes like "Twenty Flight Rock" and could do a decent imitation of Little Richard, another popular American singer at the time. Even better, Paul dared to play John a few of the songs he had written by himself on guitar, among them one called "I Lost My Little Girl." John had never written his own songs before, and seeing Paul singing and playing his own songs inspired him to write as well. It would be the beginning of a long, competitive, and incredibly productive songwriting partnership between them.

Paul and George Become Quarry Men

Paul joined John's Quarry Men almost right away and began playing small performances with them. He was a good fit with the group, since he shared so many of John's musical idols, all of them American rock and roll stars such as Buddy Holly, Chuck Berry, Little Richard, the Everly Brothers, and especially Elvis. Paul soon introduced John to a school friend of his named George Harrison. George was nearly three years younger than John, but at fifteen knew far more guitar chords than John and Paul put together. John and George didn't hit it off immediately, most likely due to the age difference. But George was eventually asked to join the Quarry Men.

George was born on February 25, 1943, in Liverpool. His parents, Harold and Louise Harrison, were loving and supportive of him throughout his childhood. According to George, "My mum did encourage me, perhaps most of all by never discouraging me from anything I wanted to do." At his request, his parents bought him a guitar at the age of fourteen, and from that point on they encouraged George to play. Practicing until his fingers bled, George picked out songs by the great skiffle bands of the time in his bedroom.

Pete Best *(far left)* joined the band right when they changed their name to the Silver Beatles.

After George joined the Quarry Men, they frequently used his parents' house to practice. On George's addition to the band, John would later say, "Meeting Paul was just like two people meeting. Not falling in love or anything. Just us. It went on. It worked. Now there were three of us who thought the same."

The New Kids

Stuart Sutcliffe, former bassist for the Beatles, had a big impact on John.

In August of 1959, the Quarry Men, at this time comprised of John, Paul, George, and another school friend, played seven shows at a new Liverpool club called the Casbah, which was owned and run by Mona Best. Her son, Pete, who was the same age as the Quarry Men, happened to play the drums in another Liverpool group called the Blackjacks. Pete Best soon left the Blackjacks to join the Quarry Men, who had, by that time, changed their name to the Silver Beatles. Two days after Pete joined the group, they would change their name to the Beatles. Their name would never change again.

In addition to John, Paul, and George on guitars and Pete on the drums, the Beatles now featured Stuart Sutcliffe on the bass guitar. Stuart was a friend of John's from art college in Liverpool, which John had been attending since 1957. Stuart was as talented a painter as he was limited as a bass player, but he had a huge influence on John's personality, being extremely creative and individualistic. Stuart would accompany the band on their first trip to Hamburg, Germany, in August 1960.

Their part-time manager, Allan Williams, had arranged the band's trip to Hamburg. Several other Liverpool pop groups managed by Allan

Fun Fact!

On several occasions, John wore a toilet seat around his neck while he played in Germany. This was just one of their attention-getting schemes—the Beatles were known for their on-stage antics.

19

Williams had been invited to Hamburg to play by a visiting German nightclub owner, and had written back indicating that the money they were earning there was good—better than they could make in Liverpool. The Beatles soon began performing shows at the Kaiserkeller Club in Hamburg. This time onstage, in the trenches, so to speak, was to have an invaluable effect on their future career as the Beatles.

Hard Times in Hamburg

Upon their arrival in Hamburg, the Beatles' living conditions were less than ideal. In fact, they were miserable. As Paul described, "We lived backstage in the Bambi Kino [movie theater], next to the toilets, and you could always smell them. The room had been an old storeroom, and there were just concrete walls and nothing else. No heat, no wallpaper, not a lick of paint; and two sets of bunk beds, like little camp beds, with not very many covers. We were frozen."

Between August and September of 1960, the band played long, grueling nightly sets for the

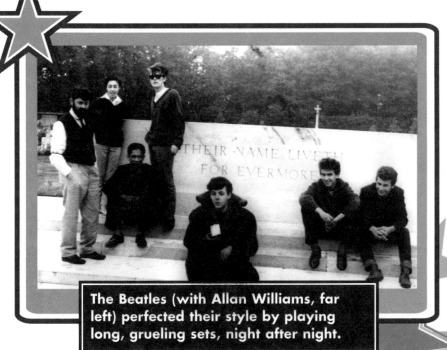

THEIR NAME LIVETH
FOR EVERMORE

The Beatles (with Allan Williams, far left) perfected their style by playing long, grueling sets, night after night.

German crowds. "We probably played four hours [per night], but we had to stretch it over an eight-hour period, and that's an awful long time to play. I mean, even bands now with three- or four-hour sets is a long time," Paul recalled. Although it was an exhausting playing routine, it sharpened their musical skills and served to tighten up the band's sound. John later said, "We'd been meek and

Paul's violin-shaped bass was a fixture during Beatles performances.

mild musicians at first; now we became a powerhouse."

Among other things they discovered in Hamburg was the ability to entertain the crowds with onstage antics. The humor and charm they would later display for millions of fans in movies and TV appearances was starting to take real shape in Germany. They had an amazing ability to attract people's attention and keep it, sometimes through any means possible. "In Hamburg we had to play for eight hours, so we really had to find a new way of playing," John recalled. "We played very loud—bang, bang all the time. The Germans loved it."

During this stay in Hamburg, the Beatles had to compete for attention with Rory Storm and

That Famous Bass

To this day, one of Paul McCartney's trademarks is his violin-shaped Hofner bass guitar. He began playing the instrument when Stuart Sutcliffe quit the Beatles to attend art college, leaving an opening for a bass player. George remembered, "At that point, I said, 'We're not going to get a fifth person in the band. One of us three is going to be the bass player, and it's not going to be me,' and Paul didn't seem to mind the idea." Paul had spotted a bass player in another Hamburg group using the Hofner bass, and he liked it so much he went out and bought one for himself. He used it on most of the Beatles' recordings, and it was always present in their live shows.

the Hurricanes, another group from Liverpool. They were known for their great live shows and professionalism on stage. Unlike the Beatles, who wore black leather and cowboy boots, Rory Storm's band wore clean, matching suits, complete with matching handkerchiefs and neckties. Their drummer was particularly noteworthy—he had a tough look about him, with a gray streak in his hair and a cocky look in his eye. His name was Ringo Starr. Ringo would often go to see the Beatles play very late at night and shout out requests. This was how they first came to know each other. Ringo would cross paths with the Beatles again in the near future, in a way that would change his life forever.

Back to Liverpool

In December, the Beatles' luck appeared to run out: George was ordered to leave Germany for being underage and working in a nightclub. Paul and Pete were also asked to leave the country for allegedly starting a fire in their rooms in

Hamburg. They returned to Liverpool somewhat discouraged, but determined to keep making music their way. Their first appearance back in England was at the Casbah Club, where they had first performed a year and a half earlier. A few days later they played on a bill at the Town Hall Ballroom, and that night, as the Beatles launched into songs from their Hamburg set lists, the crowds surged forward to the stage. Their music was tight, powerful, and very catchy. The group was spellbinding, creating a sensation among the assembled teenagers. Liverpool was just getting its very first taste of what would become known around the entire world as Beatlemania.

The Beatles

1957
On July 6, Paul McCartney meets John Lennon. John invites Paul to join the Quarry Men.

1958
George Harrison joins the Quarry Men.

1960
The Beatles travel to Germany and perform long, grueling sets night after night.

1962
Ringo Starr joins the Beatles and they release "Love Me Do," their first single.

1963
The Beatles' second single, "Please Please Me," is released in Britain. It stays in the number-one slot for two weeks.

1964
On February 9, the Beatles perform on *The Ed Sullivan Show* in New York and are watched by a record-setting 73 million people.

1965
The Beatles play for a record-breaking 55,600 people at New York's Shea Stadium.

1968
The group travels to India to attend a retreat in Rishikesh. Ringo, Paul, and John leave before the retreat is over.

1966
On August 29, the Beatles give their last live concert, in San Francisco, California.

1969
On January 30, the Beatles perform together for the last time live, on the rooftop of Apple Records' London office.

1970
Paul announces publicly that he has left the Beatles.

After their return to Liverpool from Hamburg in December 1960, the Beatles found that their playing had improved, and that people had actually started to notice them: "We discovered we were quite famous," said John. "It was when we began to think for the first time that we were good. Up to Hamburg we thought we were okay, but not good enough." In Hamburg, their contract

had indicated that they needed to play from 7:00 PM until 2:00 AM, except Saturdays when they would play until 3:00. The grueling hours only seemed to make them a tougher and tighter band. George described the long Hamburg shows as the Beatles' apprenticeship, the place where they truly became musicians: "We had to learn millions of songs. We had to play so long we just played everything . . . We'd get a Chuck Berry record, and learn it all, same with Little Richard, the Everly Brothers, Buddy Holly, Fats Domino—everything." And perhaps most interesting of all, the Beatles would also make up songs of their own, to help pass those long hours onstage.

Beatle Style

On March 21, 1961, the Beatles made their first appearance at the Cavern Club in Liverpool. It was the first of many performances there that would help solidify their Liverpool audience, and ultimately open them up to a wider audience. George was now eighteen, and the following

Did You Know?

The "Beatle haircut" was courtesy of Stuart Sutcliffe. This style was long and combed down, not greased and combed up as had been the style of most rock and rollers in those days. At first the other band members laughed at this style, but gradually each adopted it. It would become the group's trademark.

month the Beatles returned to Hamburg, the first of several short return trips there that year. The Beatles' first recording was an exciting development on this trip. They backed a singer named Tony Sheridan on a song called "My Bonnie (Lies Over the Ocean)," as Tony Sheridan and the Beat Boys. The single was a hit in Germany and later released in Britain, this time as Tony Sheridan and the Beatles. John wasn't too excited about the production values: "It's just Tony Sheridan singing, with us banging in the background. It's terrible. It could be anybody." Regardless, it marked a major milestone for the band.

The Beatles often played Liverpool's Cavern Club.

When they returned to Liverpool in July 1961, a newspaper called *Mersey Beat* had appeared, dedicated to the young Liverpool groups popular at the time. The Beatles were performing a lot in clubs, building on their local following, and attracted the attention of one of the paper's writers. John, who was always the sly wit of the group, did an interview and shed some light on the group's name: "Many people ask what are Beatles? Why Beatles? Uh, Beatles, how did the name arrive? It came in a vision—a man appeared

The Beatles still had a tough, streetwise look during their gigs at the Cavern Club.

on a flaming pie and said unto them: 'From this day on you are Beatles with an A.'"

Hello Brian

Among the many people taking notice of the Beatles was Brian Epstein, who ran a Liverpool record store and was a regular record columnist for *Mersey Beat*. Several teenagers had walked into his store requesting a record called "My Bonnie" by the Beatles, which Brian regretfully said he'd never heard. His interest piqued, Brian started going down to the Cavern Club to hear them play their lunchtime sessions. They immediately struck him. "There was quite clearly enormous

The Beatles generated tremendous energy during their Cavern Club shows.

excitement. They seemed to give off some sort of personal magnetism. I was fascinated by them," he said later. Brian liked them so much that he quickly made a move to become their manager, and after very brief negotiations, he did just that.

Brian dedicated all of his energies to getting them better bookings, more money, and more fame. But most of all he wanted to get them into

33

The Beatles

Manager Brian Epstein was instrumental in making the Beatles successful.

a recording studio. His trade had been record selling, and he knew the power of a successful single. He was incredibly well-organized, and had an obvious effect on the Beatles' attitude. "Brian made it all seem real," said John. "We were just in a daydream 'til he came along." They had a failed audition with Decca Records in January of 1962, but after winning a popularity poll in *Mersey Beat*, Brian sent them back to Germany, where they played in triumph at the Star Club, the biggest Hamburg club of its kind. The Beatles were very successful but needed a hit record to push their popularity over the top. Brian found his way to George Martin, a record producer at EMI Records in London. Martin listened to the Beatles tapes and liked what he heard, particularly "Paul's voice and George's guitar playing." He agreed to give them an audition, and Brian hurriedly sent a telegram to the Beatles: CONGRATULATIONS, BOYS. EMI REQUEST RECORDING SESSION. PLEASE REHEARSE NEW MATERIAL.

Enter Ringo

Among the new songs they started writing immediately was one song called "Love Me Do," written by John and Paul. The audition on June 6, 1962, seemed to go extremely well, but they didn't hear back from George Martin immediately. In late July he contacted Brian to offer them a recording contract. But before they could record, the Beatles had to make a substantial change in their lineup: Pete Best, their drummer for two years, would have to go. Martin felt his playing wasn't solid enough for the band. It was Brian's duty to break the news to Pete. Pete later recalled the meeting: "He said George Martin wasn't too pleased with my playing. He said the boys thought I didn't

The Beatles

Ringo Starr (Richard Starkey) replaced Pete Best as the band's drummer.

fit in. But there didn't seem anything definite. At last I said, if that's the way it is, then that's it." His replacement would be Ringo Starr, the fun-loving young drummer from one of the roughest parts of Liverpool, whom the band had met during their very first stay in Hamburg.

Ringo was born Richard Starkey on July 7, 1940. His parents were both working class, and they split when Ringo was only three. Ringo, like all of the other Beatles, hadn't been particularly interested in music as a child and had not learned any instrument. When the skiffle craze set in during his teenage years, Ringo was drawn to the drums, so his father bought him a cheap drum kit. Ringo eventually became the regular drummer for Rory Storm and the Hurricanes, who, like the Beatles, had performed on Hamburg stages. It was there that Ringo first did stand-in engagements with the Beatles, and hung out with them a bit in between gigs. When the Beatles eventually offered him Pete Best's job, he was pondering an offer from another group. Luckily, the Beatles offered slightly more money, and the rest is history.

The First Singles

The Beatles first British single, "Love Me Do," with a B-side of "P.S. I Love You," ended up selling 100,000 copies in England and got them to number seventeen on the charts. It gave the group a taste of things to come. "All we had wanted was a piece of vinyl—my God, a record that you hadn't made in a booth somewhere! And now we wanted to be Number One. They were both as important," said Ringo. In December, they played two more weeks at the Star Club in Hamburg (their last trip to Hamburg ever), and began a tour of

Scotland in January—in a van. The Beatles were also put on tour along with several other groups, and covered much of England in this time. This sparked a following outside of Liverpool.

The Beatles released their second single, "Please Please Me" in February of 1963, and this became their first number-one single in Britain. They followed this quickly with their first album, also called *Please Please Me*, and their third single, "From Me To You," which also made number one. After more brief tours and a handful of TV appearances, the Beatles were starting to cause riots wherever they went. They were mobbed in the theaters where they played and at their hotels. Their fourth single, "She Loves You," another number one and their biggest yet, took them to another level. On October 13, 1963, they topped the bill on a show that was televised around the nation as *Sunday Night at the London Palladium.* The TV audience was estimated at 15 million people. The crowds outside the Palladium were hysterical, and the police had difficulty controlling them. The phenomenon called Beatlemania was now in full swing in England.

3

Beatlemania

The end of 1963 marked the Beatles' rise to international superstardom. They were now christened "The Fab Four" by the press. After their triumph at the London Palladium, the Beatles followed up with an appearance at the Royal Variety Performance, at which several members of the British royal family were in

attendance. The Beatles performed "She Loves You" and dazzled the audience there as well; no one seemed immune to their charms. Teenagers were starting to grow their hair long, like the Beatles, and Beatle wigs were selling faster than they could be made. At performances, the crowds just got wilder. At a November show in Plymouth, hoses had to be turned on screaming fans to control them, and that same week in Birmingham, the Beatles escaped from the crowds disguised as policemen. Their record sales had gone through the roof, aided by their fifth single, "I Want to Hold Your Hand," and the release of their second album *With the Beatles*, with its famous black-and-white cover photograph. *With the Beatles* received the most advanced orders for any album up until that time.

The Beatles had clearly outgrown Liverpool. Each of them gradually moved to London, which was the cultural center of England. "Our lives were changing," George said. "The way that we measured success or wealth now was that we had motorcars and lived in Mayfair and had four suits when we traveled. That was not bad really." None

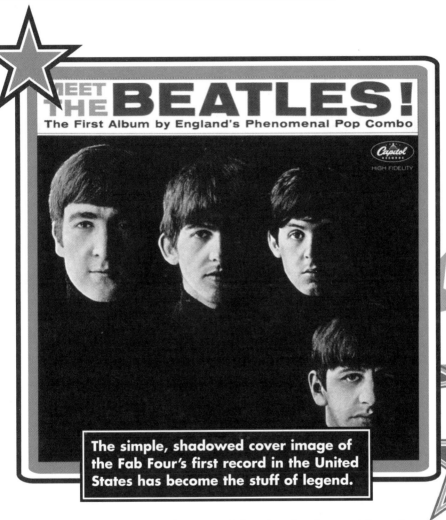

MEET THE **BEATLES!**

The First Album by England's Phenomenal Pop Combo

Capitol
RECORDS
HIGH FIDELITY

The simple, shadowed cover image of the Fab Four's first record in the United States has become the stuff of legend.

of the Beatles, or George Martin, had any idea that this fan adulation and wild success would last. As George Martin recalled, "It was very difficult in

Beatle Hair, Beatle Boots

Among the many changes the Beatles brought to the world were several fashion styles—their clothes and hair. Their hairstyle got them referred to as "Mop Tops" and that wasn't inaccurate: The style was very long for a time in which crew cuts and flattops ruled. Many Americans in particular considered the Beatles' hair a sort of bizarre gimmick. To millions of others, however, it was a simple, liberating, and daring idea. Throughout the rest of the sixties, hairstyles, especially for men, got longer and longer.

Another Beatle trademark was their fondness for pointed leather boots, which all four of them wore. The shoes were hip and seemed a sort of holdover from their rougher Hamburg days. They can still be found in some shoe stores today, and are still known as Beatle boots.

Beatle fans all over the world were spending their money on Beatle wigs to show their devotion.

1963 to think the Beatles were going to last forever and that I would be talking about them thirty years on." George Martin turned out to be instrumental in their eventual success in the United States. He had sent the first four Beatles singles—three of the four number ones in Britain—to his counterpart in the United States, telling him how fantastic the group was and how he had to issue the records in the United States. But each single was turned down, with the explanation that they weren't any good and just wouldn't succeed in the States. Meanwhile, the *Sunday Times* in Britain had christened them "the greatest composers since Beethoven." It was just a matter of time before America opened its arms to the Beatles.

They Want to Hold Your Hand

"I Want to Hold Your Hand" was finally released in the United States in January 1964, and it moved up the charts quickly. The Beatles were playing a three-week stand in Paris when they got the news that "I Want to Hold Your Hand" had gone to number one in the United States. Soon enough, *Meet the Beatles,* the same album that in Britain had been titled *With the Beatles,* hit number one on the U.S. album charts. In February, the Beatles made their first visit to the States, touching down at Kennedy airport with more than 10,000 screaming teenagers greeting them. All eyes were glued to this British phenomenon called the Beatles.

The next single, "Can't Buy Me Love," went straight to number one in the United States and

The Beatles were always greeted by thousands of hysterical fans wherever they arrived.

Britain. The advance sales alone on this single were three million, a world record. At one time the group had the top five records on the charts! They began filming their first movie, *A Hard Day's Night* (Ringo supplied the title), in March. "In 1964, we seemed to fit a week into every day," said George. The film was a huge success on both sides of the

Did You Know?

The Beatles played *The Ed Sullivan Show* in New York, to an estimated TV audience of 73 million. Hunter Davies, in his official biography of the Beatles, reported: "The screams echoed across America. In New York, during the show, not one hubcap from a car was stolen. Throughout America, not one major crime was committed by a teenager."

Atlantic, and featured a soundtrack written entirely by the Beatles. John and Paul had to race to compose the soundtrack music for the film, and among the brilliant songs was the title song, with its opening chiming guitar chord. That chord seemed to announce the presence of something young and entirely new, something important enough to stay around for a while.

A World Apart

It is worthwhile to note how different the Beatles were from other groups at the time, and not just in terms of their mammoth popularity. By the time *A Hard Day's Night* was emerging, they were writing and performing all of their own songs. Until this time, songwriting was considered out of the range of most pop stars; most pop singers simply rearranged other writers' songs for their hits. Beatles' songs were also very consistent and incredibly catchy, even the songs that would end up on the B-sides of singles. The songs were varied enough to offer something for almost everybody, which was a key to their

A Hard Day's Night was the Beatles' first film.

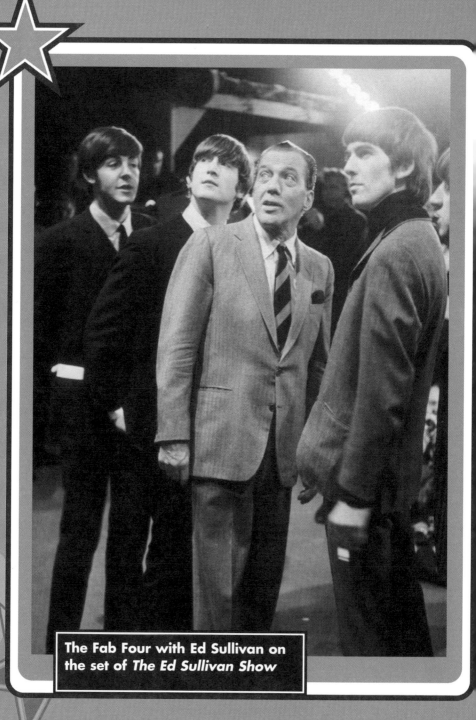

The Fab Four with Ed Sullivan on the set of *The Ed Sullivan Show*

popularity. Their audience reached further than just the teenage crowd, and into all age ranges. The Beatles were clearly more than the sum of their parts: They were four distinct personalities, each of which made a vital contribution to the whole. Most pop groups at the time typically featured one main star with some nameless side players. Not so with the Beatles.

They closed out 1964 with an enormous tour of the United States—twenty-four cities, 24,441 miles, and thirty performances. Even with all of their unbelievable, unprecedented success, it all began to slowly take its toll on the group. They had lost some of the initial euphoria at achieving such heights. Moving from venue to venue, they would be trapped in their dressing rooms. Policemen and bodyguards had to escort them to their hotels, and they rarely went out in public alone, if at all. By any account, they were essentially living in a fishbowl. Most of the next two years of their career would be dominated by touring. The touring life so controlled their world that they eventually decided to move away from it completely to focus on their next frontier: perfecting their recorded sound.

4

An End and a Beginning

Fame was having its effect on each Beatle by late 1964. The initial novelty of the mass hysteria they had caused was wearing off, leaving them dazed in the settling dust. They had certainly inspired frenzied excitement in a very short period of time. For instance, 300,000 people had greeted them when they arrived in Adelaide, Australia, during their world tour; only a year or so earlier, the four of them had been touring northern England in a freezing van, huddled together for warmth. Touring itself had become a prison for them, and each concert, usually lasting only thirty minutes, was completely drowned out by the screams of the crowds. In the absence of today's high-quality sound systems, most of the fans at their shows could only see the group's lips moving, not really hearing them at all. Paul, always looking on the bright side, would later say that all the screaming "covered a multitude of sins: we were out of tune. It didn't matter—we couldn't hear it, nor could they."

The End of Touring Life

George noted that their musicianship began to suffer as a result of the prolonged touring—and screaming. "There was no satisfaction in it. Nobody could hear. It was just a bloody big row. We got worse as musicians, playing the same old junk everyday." John, always questioning and uncompromising by nature, also began to feel at

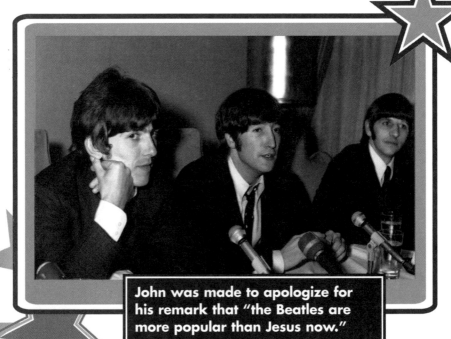

John was made to apologize for his remark that "the Beatles are more popular than Jesus now."

odds with his fame. "People think fame and money bring freedom but they don't," he explained. "We're more conscious now of the limitations it places on us rather than the freedom. We can't even spend the allowance we get, because there's nothing to spend it on. What can you spend [it] on in a room? When you're on tour, you exist in this kind of vacuum

More Popular than Jesus?

A huge public furor erupted in the United States over a remark John made to a British newspaper writer. In the interview, he had said that the Beatles "are more popular than Jesus now." Taken out of context, the remark caused riots and mass Beatles record burnings all over the United States, especially in the South. The Beatles were stalked by Ku Klux Klan members outside many of their shows and received many threats. John, quite scared, eventually apologized publicly for the remark. Although it wasn't the only reason, the incident did contribute to the group's decision to stop touring in 1966.

all the time." The Beatles would continue to tour the world throughout 1965 and 1966, including a famous show at Shea Stadium in New York in the summer of 1965, at which nearly 56,000 people showed up! They

An astounding 56,000 people showed up on August 15, 1965, to watch the Beatles play New York City's Shea Stadium.

played what would be their last British show in early 1966. In August 1966, at a show in Candlestick Park in San Francisco, they had reached a unanimous decision. "We knew," recalled George, "this is it—we're not going to do this again. This is the last concert." That night the Beatles took photographs of themselves on stage to mark the occasion. It was truly the end of an era, but the beginning of an even more important phase of their lives.

Inventions

Throughout their touring years, the Beatles released a succession of singles and albums that marked them as an innovative force in the recording studio. "I Feel Fine" was a single that featured a short burst of high-pitched noise at it's beginning, which turned out to be the first deliberate guitar feedback ever used on a record. "Help!" the title song from the soundtrack and film of the same name, was a confessional song written by John which illustrated his state of mind in the wake of Beatlemania:

When I was younger, so much younger
than today,
I never needed anybody's help in any way.
But now these days are gone, I'm not so
self-assured,
Now I find I've changed my mind and opened
up the doors.

"Norwegian Wood," from their *Rubber Soul* album, featured a sitar, which is an Indian instrument shaped somewhat like an elongated guitar. "Yesterday," a Paul composition, was the first Beatles single to feature only one of the group performing—Paul, alone with a guitar.

One of the reasons for the increasing diversity of their music was the fact that John and Paul weren't writing as many songs together. In their early days they had collaborated on most of the group's songs, especially the first hit singles. Now, while they would assist each other with bits of songs—helping each other finish a musical or lyrical part they were stuck on—most of the ideas would come from one or the other of them. Still, it was obvious that Lennon

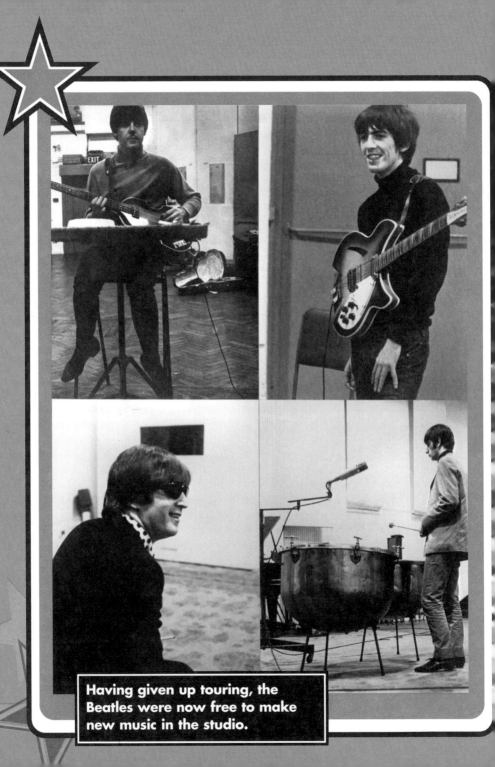

Having given up touring, the Beatles were now free to make new music in the studio.

and McCartney, the core songwriters, were very well matched. "Part of the secret collaboration," recalled Paul, "was that we liked each other. He'd sing something and I'd say 'Yeah' and trade off on that."

New Sounds

On a track like "Tomorrow Never Knows," recorded for their landmark 1966 album, *Revolver,* it was obvious that their sound was becoming increasingly complex. On this particular song each Beatle created a tape loop to use in the song's background, and the effect was a pattern of birdlike sounds. The song itself was based around one chord. Although it sounds very simple, the song has an immediate and surprising effect. "'Tomorrow Never Knows' was a great innovation," said George Martin, their producer. "John wanted a very spooky kind of track, a very ethereal sound." "Eleanor Rigby" is another haunting track from the same album, and features Paul singing about a lonely spinster, backed only by a string quartet. The Beatles' minds were opening up to new influences, which were translating into new ideas all the time. The confidence they had earned with their endless parade of hit singles was now directed toward experimenting with any new sound they could come up with. However unusual the sound, from a tape loop to a sitar, it was always in the service of a great, catchy song.

With touring now at an end, and the groundbreaking *Revolver* album just behind them, the Beatles took a small break in late 1966. George went to India to study the sitar. Paul worked on making movie soundtrack music. John decided to accept an offer to appear in a movie called *How I Won the War*, directed by Richard Lester, who also had directed *A Hard Day's Night*. While on location in Spain, John started to write an unusual and very personal song, "Strawberry Fields Forever." The lyrics referred in part to a Salvation Army home in Liverpool called Strawberry Fields, and so invoked John's childhood memories. It started out as a simple song played on guitar, but once back in Abbey Road Studios it grew into much more. It became one of the most powerful songs of the psychedelic period of the 1960s. The term "psychedelic" came from the popularity of mind-expanding drugs like LSD, which many claimed opened up the mind's locked imaginative powers. Together with Paul's song "Penny Lane" as the B-side of the single, "Strawberry Fields Forever" became one of the most innovative singles ever, and remains so to this day.

Making a Masterpiece

The Beatles went into the Abbey Road Studios for an intense six months of recording. Paul had come in with a song called "Sgt. Pepper's Lonely Hearts Club Band," and the group decided to build an entire record around it. "We would be Sgt. Pepper's band, and for the whole of the album we'd pretend to be someone else. It liberated you—you could do anything when you got to the mike or on your guitar, because it wasn't you," Paul said later. The record itself was released in June of 1967. George Martin recalled that the record astonished the entire pop music world, including him. "Nothing remotely like *Pepper* had been heard before. It came at a time when people were thirsty for something new, but its newness still caught them by surprise. It certainly caught me on the hop!" He added: "Up until this point, the Beatles had been pretty much bubble-gum artists. With *Pepper* they drew a line and crossed it."

That crossing was demonstrated with tracks like "Lucy in the Sky with Diamonds," with its impressionistic lyrics, and "Being for the Benefit of Mr. Kite," with its swirling sound effects and circus appeal. "A Day in the Life," the

Fun Fact!

The Beatles used a symphony orchestra for "A Day in the Life," the closing song of their masterpiece, *Sgt. Pepper's Lonely Hearts Club Band.* When the session began, the Beatles passed out novelties for the members of the orchestra to wear: red noses, colored glasses, and a monkey's paw for the violin player!

record's concluding song, boasted a forty-one-piece orchestra creating a massive, thundering swell at two points in the song. The album's cover also made history of a kind; it featured the Beatles in the colorful uniforms of a marching band (the Pepper band) surrounded by paper cutouts of some of their personal heroes, among them Groucho Marx, W.C. Fields, and Bob Dylan. The album also marked the first time in history that a group had printed their lyrics on an album sleeve. A simple idea, but much imitated since then. The Beatles had clearly made the right decision in choosing the studio over touring, if the quality of the work on *Sgt. Pepper* was any indication. In dedicating their efforts exclusively toward recording, they had committed to extending the possibilities they found there, and as a result their ideas are still heard on records by other artists being released today.

5

1967–1968

In 1967, the Beatles reached their high-water mark as a creative force in pop music. With *Sgt. Pepper's Lonely Hearts Club Band*, they had blown away all competition with a brilliant record, full of melody, imagery, and musical invention. The record took on a life of its own, becoming a

cultural phenomenon and one of the most important achievements of the 1960s. At the time, it seemcd that nothing could stop their stay at the summit of fame and success. But there was an event in the summer of 1967 that in many ways would mark the beginning of the end of the Beatles, an end that wouldn't formally occur until three years later. It was thc death of their manager, Brian Epstein, of a drug overdose. Agreeing that no one could possibly replace Brian, the Beatles chose not to find a new manager, at least for the time being.

Another Tour, Sort Of

The Beatles were still resistant to public performances, but in late 1967 they had made a TV film called *Magical Mystery Tour* to accompany six new songs they had written. *Magical Mystery Tour* was originally an idea of Paul's. The group wrote, directed, acted in, and edited the film, in which they travel around remote parts of England with a busload of characters, from dancers to circus freaks, essentially to see what would happen. What did happen wasn't very interesting. The whole venture was poorly planned and overly ambitious at a time in which they were keenly feeling the absence of a manager. The premiere of this film marked some of the first truly negative reviews that the group had received since they had hit the big time in 1963. Though not anywhere near as successful as *Sgt. Pepper* had been, it did at least manage to keep them in the public eye.

In the wake of *Magical Mystery Tour,* the group once again turned to other pursuits. George was the one Beatle who had become interested in Indian music and spirituality

Fun Fact!

On June 25, 1967, the Beatles appeared on the live TV special *Our World.* They performed a song they had specially written, called "All You Need Is Love," for a worldwide audience of 350 million people.

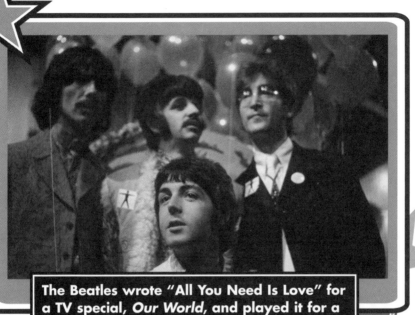

The Beatles wrote "All You Need Is Love" for a TV special, *Our World*, and played it for a broadcast audience of 350 million people.

over time. He had introduced the other Beatles to the Maharishi Mahesh Yogi, an Indian guru who would briefly become the group's meditation teacher. The entire group eventually attended a lengthy retreat in Rishikesh, India, in early 1968. Ringo, Paul, and John left the retreat before it ended, each feeling that in the end, meditation

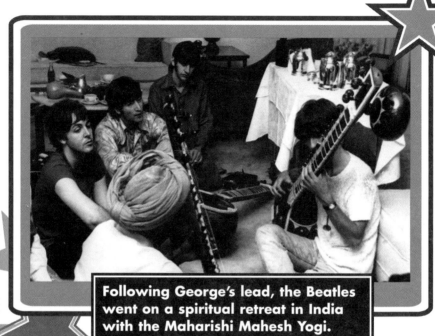

Following George's lead, the Beatles went on a spiritual retreat in India with the Maharishi Mahesh Yogi.

wasn't right for them. George was the only Beatle left believing in meditation's gifts. This trip marked the last time the Beatles ever traveled together as a group. Each Beatle seemed to be developing an increasingly strong individual identity, and this was ultimately reflected in their songs.

A White Album?

Their time in India had been far from wasted:
They had accumulated a backlog of thirty-four
songs, almost all of which had been written
there. All of the songs were recorded, one of
them being "Hey Jude," which was the longest-
ever pop single at over seven minutes. Thirty of
the songs made it onto a two-record set called
The Beatles, released in autumn 1968. Its famous
cover was plain white; fans would call it simply
The White Album. It was the longest full-length
album released by a major rock artist up until
that time. On this record, the Beatles had begun
working together a little differently. Each band
member worked independently, with minimal
help from the others.

Overall, the record shows that the Beatles'
musical imaginations were wide open, even
though the sound is much different from *Sgt.
Pepper*. There are fewer sound effects, and much
less recording trickery. "Ob-La-Di, Ob-La-Da" is
light and poppy, while "Martha My Dear" is about

John's girlfriend Yoko Ono's presence during the *White Album* recordings caused friction with the rest of the band.

Paul's sheepdog, Martha. "The Continuing Story of Bungalow Bill" is a lighthearted John Lennon song about a safari hunter; "Good Night" is a lullaby John wrote for his son Julian. Some of the songs are darker-edged, such as John's "Happiness Is a Warm Gun" and Paul's "Helter Skelter." It was as if the Beatles were trying to touch on nearly every element in popular music on one album, and it worked. While less focused than other Beatles records, *The White Album* showed they were still highly inventive. One of the most notable events surrounding the album was the presence of John's new girlfriend (soon to be his second wife), Yoko Ono, in the studio during the sessions. An artist whom John had met in 1966 at a London art gallery, Yoko quickly swept John off his feet and into a new period of creativity. "Whatever I went through was worth it to meet Yoko, so if I had to do all the things I did in my life—which is have a troubled childhood, a troubled teenage and an amazing whirlwind life with the Beatles, and then finally coming to land meeting Yoko—it was worth it," John said.

John and Yoko's relationship would be much-publicized in the coming years, but its immediate effects on the Beatles were apparent. Her presence in the studio marked the first time a Beatle girlfriend or wife had been allowed into the sessions. She sat quietly by John's side during nearly every recording. While it caused some unease among the other members, it was clear that she was there to stay. John said, "Yoko really woke me up to myself. She didn't fall in love with the Beatle, she didn't fall in love with the fame. She fell in love with me for myself, and through that brought out the best in me."

Submarines and Meanies

The Beatles attended the London premiere of a new animated film called *Yellow Submarine* in July 1968. The film marked the end of the Beatles psychedelic phase, but interestingly it does not feature their voices (other actors did their voices in the film), and the soundtrack features only four new songs. The film itself is a funny, nonsensical, colorful fantasy set to previously recorded Beatle music. The Beatles only participation was a "live" appearance as themselves at the end of the film, basically to say "thanks" for watching the film. The whole package was an opportunity to market more Beatles merchandise, from Blue Meanie stickers to wristwatches. (Blue Meanies were the fictional villains in the film.)

Ringo and George are menaced by one of the Blue Meanies from the film *Yellow Submarine*.

The premiere marked the last time the group was mobbed by hysterical crowds. The group themselves approved of the production. "I liked the film. I think it's a classic," said George. "That film works for every generation— every baby, three, four years old, goes through *Yellow Submarine*."

Beatles, Inc.

At the time, it did still seem as though the Beatles could do little wrong. With a sense of optimism, they launched their own company, called Apple Corps, which included a record label that would release all of the Beatles future recordings, as well as those of some promising up-and-comers (among them James Taylor). *The White Album* was the first record released on their label. Although built on a great idea—to create a place where artists with talent could come to make records without having to make a record deal with a major company—Apple quickly buckled under the weight of too many ideas and too small a grip on reality. The company quickly lost lots of money, primarily because there was no one who was serious about running it. John recalled, "People were robbing us and living on us to the tune of eighteen or twenty thousand pounds a week that was rolling out of Apple and nobody was doing anything about it." Later in 1969, disagreements over Apple would be an indirect cause to the start of the Beatles breakup.

Ringo Quits the Beatles!

On August 22, 1968, during sessions for *The White Album,* Ringo decided to leave the Beatles, feeling that tensions among the group had grown too high for him to keep working. He was gone for nearly two weeks (a time in which the group did try to keep recording without him, with Paul filling in on drums), when he was finally persuaded by all of the other Beatles to come back. Returning to the studio, he found his drums had been covered in flowers by the band.

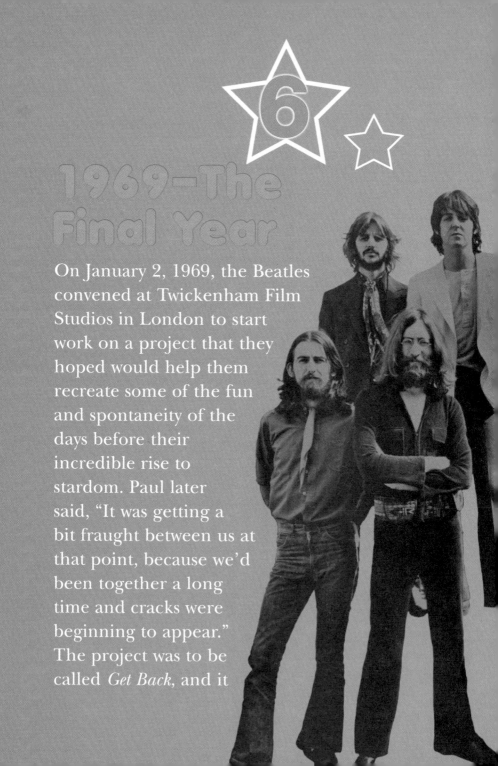

6

1969—The Final Year

On January 2, 1969, the Beatles convened at Twickenham Film Studios in London to start work on a project that they hoped would help them recreate some of the fun and spontaneity of the days before their incredible rise to stardom. Paul later said, "It was getting a bit fraught between us at that point, because we'd been together a long time and cracks were beginning to appear." The project was to be called *Get Back*, and it was partially intended to satisfy Paul's strong desire to have the group play in front of an audience again. It would become a film and an album—actually, a film of the band making a new live album. Coming as it did only eleven weeks after they had finished recording *The White Album*, in which different working styles and interpersonal tensions had steadily risen to the surface, the film project may not have come at the best time.

Inner Strife

John, now happy in his still-new relationship with Yoko Ono, began to look at the Beatles as less an inspiration than an obligation. It was obvious that a lot of his old enthusiasm for musical discovery had left him. As he explained, "I just made the records with the Beatles like one goes to one's job at nine in the morning. Paul or whoever would say, 'It's time to make a record.' I'd just go in and make a record, and not think too much about it." As it turned out, the film that would eventually be titled *Let It Be* became more a portrait of a band falling apart at the seams than a documentary of an album in the making. "I'd talked them into *Let It Be*," Paul said. "Then we had terrible arguments—so we'd get the breakup of the Beatles on film instead of what we really wanted. It was probably a better story—a sad story, but there you are." George began to feel particularly stifled by the group, since he had started writing more songs on his own, only to find it difficult to get them accepted by the others. Paul and George were especially at odds, with George feeling that Paul had become too domineering and critical of his guitar playing. George briefly left the band during the sessions, to be coaxed back soon after.

Up on the Roof

The Beatles moved the film shoot back to their own recording studios later the same month. Looking for a way to end the film, the group decided to do a concert on the roof of their studios. Thinking they would just perform the

The rooftop concert during the
sessions for *Let It Be*

songs they had been working on in the previous weeks, they began playing at lunchtime on a cold, windy day on the roof. They quickly attracted the attention of their neighbors, as well as passersby on the street. They also got the attention of the police, who soon made their way to the rooftop. "I think they pulled the plug, and that was the end of the film," said Paul. The rooftop concert turned out to be one of the Beatles' most memorable moments as a group, with all four coming together as before, singing harmonies, and playing well. It is easily the most inspired part of the film, and helps it to end on a lighter note.

Once the dust settled on the sessions, the net result was hours of audiotape and a month's worth of film, all of which had to be sorted out. Although there was an attempt made to make a proper album out of the tapes, the Beatles weren't pleased with the results and decided to shelve the project for the time being. It wouldn't be released as an album for over a year. The album, titled *Let It Be*, is probably the

Paul married Linda Eastman, an American photographer, in 1969.

Beatles' least successful album, but it is marked by some beautiful songwriting, including John's "Across the Universe" and Paul's "Get Back" and "Let It Be." It has a rougher, more spontaneous feeling than most of the other Beatle albums, which was what they had originally intended. Even though a great deal of tension had developed within the band, it was obvious that their creativity hadn't been hopelessly damaged. More proof of this creativity would turn up on their final, and most polished, record, *Abbey Road*, which they soon began to record.

John and Paul had both gotten married in March; Paul to Linda Eastman, an American photographer, and John to Yoko Ono. John and Yoko, ever the idealists, had decided to undertake a campaign for world peace. They used the publicity gained by their wedding to stage what they called "Bed-Ins for Peace" from their honeymoon hotel suite in

Fun Fact!

John documented his wedding to Yoko and its subsequent events in a single called "The Ballad of John and Yoko." It was hurriedly recorded using only Paul as his accompaniment.

Amsterdam. Assuming that the hungry press would record their every move, they decided that their space in print might as well be occupied by the theme of peace. For seven days, they remained in bed, talking day and night to reporters about the benefits of lasting peace in the world.

Through the spring and summer, as the Beatles were gradually recording the songs that would comprise their final record, it was increasingly clear that they were in the position of being nearly out of money. In spite of their being the most successful group in the history of recorded sound, Apple was losing money at an astonishing rate due to mismanagement. In attempting to solve this problem, their differences surfaced yet again, this time in their indecision over a new manager to sort out their finances. Paul wanted to use his father-in-law, Lee Eastman, while the other Beatles, especially John, were more impressed by Allen Klein, an American music manager who had helped make the Rolling Stones rich. In the end, the disputes worsened and led to the

The cover of *Abbey Road* is one of the most famous album covers in history.

conclusion that the group was in serious trouble and could be heading for a final split. But not before they made one last great musical statement.

The Last Waltz

Abbey Road, released on October 1, 1969, featured a sprinkling of everything in the Beatles' arsenal: a sweet (and huge-selling) love song in George's "Something"; John's experimental "I Want You (She's So Heavy)"; the amazingly catchy "Here Comes the Sun"; and even a children's song by Ringo called "Octopus's Garden." Most strikingly of all, the second side of the album contained a suite of songs, short pieces threaded together without gaps. It has a wonderful effect, and it culminates fittingly with "The End," a song that features the only drum solo ever on a Beatles record, as well as some dueling guitar solos from John, George, and Paul. In all, the record was the perfect ending to their recording career. As George put it: "I didn't know at the time that it was the last Beatle record that we would make, but it felt as if we were reaching the end of the line."

Abbey Road sold five million copies in the United States alone, two million more than *Sgt. Pepper's Lonely Hearts Club Band.* Among the many reasons for the huge success of the final Beatles album was a series of rumors about Paul McCartney being dead. Obsessive fans had claimed they'd found secrets hidden in Beatle lyrics that made reference to Paul having been dead since the time of *Sgt. Pepper's Lonely Hearts Club Band.* Some of these fans resorted to playing the records backwards, where they claimed they could hear the secret messages. One of the most famous "clues" came right off of the *Abbey Road* album cover: a car on the street the Beatles are crossing bears the license plate "28 IF." Fans claimed this was deliberate and meant that Paul would have been twenty-eight years old if he had lived. Of course, none of it was true—Paul was alive and well. "Paul McCartney couldn't die without the world knowing it. It's impossible—he can't go on holiday without the world knowing it. It's just insanity—but it's a great plug for *Abbey Road,*" John said later.

Once the *Abbey Road* recordings were done, John felt he had reached the end of his creative and personal rope with the band, and made it clear to the other Beatles that he wanted a "divorce." He was becoming much more interested in other projects and had formed a side group called the Plastic Ono Band, which featured Yoko Ono. He played a concert with them in Toronto, which was captured on the live album *Live Peace in Toronto.* The other Beatles encouraged John not to publicly share his feelings about breaking up the Beatles, for the time being. Even though John expressed a desire to break up the band, he did leave the door open for future collaborations with them. On August 22, 1969, the Beatles all gathered at John's house for what turned out to be the last photographs ever taken of them as a group.

And in the End

Although it had been slow in coming about, the end of the Beatles finally came in April 1970. Paul had secretly recorded his first solo album, titled simply *McCartney*. In the course of promoting it, Paul announced to the world that there would be no new Beatles projects, because he was leaving the band. By this time, there was really no band to leave. As Paul explained, "I didn't leave the Beatles. The Beatles have left the Beatles, but no one wants to be the one to say the party's over." Strangely, one month after Paul's announcement, another Beatles album appeared on the shelves. After twelve months of wrestling with the raw materials, the *Let It Be* album and film finally premiered. The film really showed the band falling apart, while the record, according to the British music magazine *New Musical Express*, marked a "sad and tatty end to a musical fusion which wiped clean and drew again the face of pop music."

Paul Breaks Away

Although the Beatles' partnership had been dissolved, each member quickly set up a career as a solo artist. Paul's debut record, *McCartney*, didn't impress fans or critics and seemed like a halfhearted effort for such an obviously talented musician. It did include one noteworthy single in "Maybe I'm Amazed." In the next few years, he followed with two more mediocre albums

Paul continued to write and perform with Wings, which he formed with his wife, Linda.

before finally hitting his old stride again with the *Band on the Run* album, recorded in 1974 with his backing band Wings (which included his wife, Linda). This featured two hit singles in "Jet" and the title song, and sold more than five million copies, making it the most popular of any of the Beatles' solo albums. Paul was ultimately the most successful ex-Beatle, with a total of seven number-one albums and nine number-one singles to his credit.

Paul continued to tour the world throughout the 1970s with and without his band Wings, but was always joined onstage by his wife, Linda, from whom he was inseparable. In more recent years, Paul has composed several classical music pieces, written and starred in a film (*Give My Regards to Broad Street*), and closed the massive 1985 Live Aid benefit concert with a version of "Let it Be." During the performance, his microphone was not working, but Paul didn't even notice it, with the crowd singing so loudly. Paul is still active in music—his last album, *Run Devil Run*, was released in 1999—and recently he appeared at the Cavern Club in Liverpool, the Beatles' old haunt in their early days. Sadly, Linda died in 1998 after a long struggle with cancer.

George's World

George's first solo album, *All Things Must Pass*, released in late 1970, would become his most famous album. It was a three-record set and

George Harrison organized and played during a benefit for famine-stricken Bangladesh.

featured the single "My Sweet Lord," which would hit number one in several countries, including the United States and Great Britain. While easily one of George's most memorable songs, "My Sweet Lord" would later cause George to be taken to court, accused of copying the melody of "He's So Fine," a song by the Chiffons from the early 1960s.

He lost the lawsuit and eventually had to pay back some of the money he had earned from the song. In 1971, George organized and performed in the Concert for Bangladesh, which also featured performances by some of his musician friends such as Bob Dylan and Eric Clapton. The show was to benefit the people of Bangladesh, who were suffering from famine and disease. It was a massive success and resulted in an album of the show, which also sold extremely well. George's next solo effort, *Living in the Material World,* contained the number-one single "Give Me Love."

George has always been the most private and introspective Beatle. He was the one most uncomfortable with his fame and the invasion of privacy it often brought. "There was more good than evil in being a Beatle," he said, "but it was awful being on the front page of everyone's life, every day." As a result, he kept recording but did go into a sort of semiretirement in the late 1970s and early 1980s, emerging in 1987 with the number one single "Got My Mind Set on You." The next year he joined the Traveling Wilburys,

Did You Know?

In 1999, an intruder broke into George's mansion outside of London and attacked him, stabbing him three times in the chest. He recovered from the injuries, but has maintained his privacy since the incident.

which included his friends Bob Dylan and Tom Petty, and recorded an album with them, which made it to number three. A follow-up album made it to number eleven. Most recently, he rerecorded "My Sweet Lord" for inclusion on an anniversary rerelease of his album, *All Things Must Pass*, in 2001.

Unfortunately, George has dealt with a number of health problems in recent years. He was treated for throat cancer in 1997 and had a cancerous lump removed from one of his lungs in 2001. It was also reported that he was undergoing treatment for a brain tumor that year. Unfortunately, George's health problems escalated, and he died of cancer on November 29, 2001.

Ringo the Great

Ringo, meanwhile, enjoyed almost immediate solo success after the Beatles breakup, recording several

Ringo continued to act in such films as *Caveman*.

albums (handling the singing himself), including his 1973 album, *Ringo*. This was his greatest commercial success, featuring songs by each of his three ex-bandmates and boasting the number-one singles "Photograph" and "You're Sixteen." He also enjoyed success in the movies, acting in films like *The Magic Christian*, *That'll be the Day*, and *Caveman*. It was during the filming of *Caveman* that he met his current wife,

95

Barbara Bach. Ringo still tours with a band he calls the All-Starr Band, and regularly performs "With a Little Help from My Friends" (from *Sgt. Pepper*) during his shows.

In terms of Ringo's career with the Beatles, it is easy to overlook many of his achievements. In the early days of their success, Ringo was the most outgoing Beatle. He was always smiling, always joking, always keeping things upbeat through the long touring days. While his role did change after touring ended, Ringo never tried to overshadow the other members of the group, choosing instead to stay quietly in the background. Ringo was always there, always supportive of the others in the group, and always ready to play. His playing, while underrated by some critics, was always right for the song. John commented, "Ringo was the greatest rock and roll drummer I ever saw."

John the Dreamer

John's first post-Beatle record, *John Lennon/Plastic Ono Band,* had a raw, loose sound and its follow-up, *Imagine,* is still considered his finest record and one of the best albums of the decade. The title song particularly seemed to sum up his feelings about peace, unity, and openness across the world:

> *You may say I'm a*
> *dreamer,*
> *But I'm not the*
> *only one.*
> *I hope someday you'll*
> *join us,*
> *And the world will*
> *live as one.*

Fans pay tribute to their slain hero, John Lennon.

John would go on to have an erratic musical and personal life for the rest of the 1970s. He settled in New York City with Yoko Ono in the early part of the decade, and would stay there for the rest of his life. In 1974, he enjoyed a number-one single with "Whatever Gets You Through the Night," but he

The Beatles and the Stones

The Rolling Stones were an up-and-coming young rock and roll band in the early 1960s, along with the Beatles. Although it's a little-known fact, the Beatles were very helpful in getting the Rolling Stones their first recording contract. At a party, George Harrison had run into some record executives who asked him who the good groups were, and he replied, "You want to get the Rolling Stones." The Beatles (actually John and Paul) donated a song to the Stones, who recorded "I Wanna Be Your Man" in 1963 and made it a British hit. All through the 1960s, the press tried to make it appear as if there was a big rivalry between the two bands, but Paul noted that it was just "newspaper talk." The Beatles and the Stones remained close over time and frequently inspired each other.

separated from Yoko for a year and went through a battle with alcohol and drugs. When he and Yoko reunited the following year, they became the parents of a baby boy named Sean. John decided to leave music for a while to become a full-time father. He had made ten albums since leaving the Beatles, and decided it was time for a rest. It ended up being nearly five years before he went back into the studio with Yoko Ono to make the *Double Fantasy* album in 1980.

On December 8, 1980, while returning home from the recording studio, John was shot dead in front of his New York City apartment building by Mark Chapman, a deranged fan. The tragedy was mourned across the world; John, through his music with the Beatles and on his own, had been such a significant part of so many people's lives. Today there is a memorial to John in Central Park in New York City, called Strawberry Fields.

All My Friends Were Beatles

Looking back on the breakup of the Beatles, George Martin, who as their record producer

The Beatles, along with producer George Martin (pictured here), changed the face of popular music.

had seen so many events from the inside, felt that it was inevitable. "They'd always been having to consider the group," he explained, "so they were a prisoner of that—and I think they eventually got fed up with it . . . They wanted to live life like other people." Even though they had all outgrown the Beatles, each one would look fondly back at his time in the group. "I felt with us four it was magical and it was telepathy," said Ringo. "When we were working in the studio sometimes it was just . . . it's indescribable, really." Summing up the closeness of the four, John said, "All my friends were the Beatles, anyway." Paul had similar feelings: "It helped that we were like a gang together. Mick Jagger [of the Rolling Stones] called us the Four-Headed Monster because we went everywhere together, dressed similarly."

It is hard to imagine that if the Beatles had not been such good friends, their partnership would have lasted so long or been so successful. Being so close, and so musically like-minded, helped them to make some of the most timeless and important pop music ever recorded. Maybe all they had done was sing and play music, but they had also managed to change something in the way people saw the world. People who liked their music also saw something special in them; the Beatles felt right for their times. More than bringing long hair and Beatle boots to the world, they brought a sense of optimism and joy at a time when it was needed. "I think we gave some sort of freedom to the world," Paul McCartney explained, "I meet

a lot of people now who say the Beatles freed them up . . . I think that the brutal honesty the Beatles had was important. So sticking to our own guns and really saying what we thought in some way gave some other people in the world the idea that they too could be truthful and get away with it, and in fact it was a good thing."

In the end, the Beatles got their wish to be the biggest rock act of all time. It may have cost them some of their own personal freedom—especially during the touring days when they were trapped in their hotel rooms—but to each of them it had been worth it. "I was glad things got as big as they did," recalled John, "because when we got nearly big, people started saying to us: 'You're the biggest thing since . . .' I got fed up that we were the biggest thing 'since.' I wanted the Beatles to just be the biggest thing. It's like gold. The more you get, the more you want."

The Beatles were a rare group whose popularity equaled their excellence as musicians and songwriters. Their music stands the test of time, and is still heard all over the radio today;

"Yesterday" has been played on the radio a record seven million times since its release. Their popularity is almost unchanged since the time of their breakup. It is hard to imagine that there are places in the world that have never heard of the Beatles and their music. George Harrison sums up the Beatles' continuing musical importance quite well: "If you listen to the music that's going on now, all the good stuff is stolen from the Beatles. Most of the good licks and riffs or ideas and [song] titles. The Beatles have been plundered for thirty years." And, no doubt, they will continue to be plundered happily by musicians and fans everywhere, for as long as there is music.

DISCOGRAPHY & FILMOGRAPHY

Selected Discography

1963 *Please Please Me*

1963 *With the Beatles*

1963 *A Hard Day's Night*

1964 *Beatles For Sale*

1965 *Help!*

1965 *Rubber Soul*

1966 *Revolver*

1967 *Sgt. Pepper's Lonely Heart's Club Band*

1967 *Magical Mystery Tour*

1968 *The Beatles (The White Album)*

1969 *Yellow Submarine*

1969 *Abbey Road*

1970 *Let It Be*

Selected Filmography

1964 *A Hard Day's Night*

1965 *Help!*

1967 *Magical Mystery Tour*

1969 *Yellow Submarine*

GLOSSARY

apprenticeship A period of learning a trade or art by studying under an experienced person.

bass guitar A four-string guitar that plays lower notes than a traditional six-string guitar.

beat groups Name for Liverpool groups with a certain rock and roll sound in the early 1960s.

Beatlemania The worldwide hysteria created by the Beatles in the years 1963–1966.

feedback Noise created by guitar amplifiers, usually when a plugged-in electric guitar is held too close to the plugged-in amplifier.

guru Indian word for a teacher or spiritual guide.

individualistic A personality trait marked by independent thought and actions.

phenomenon A significant thing or event that defies scientific explanation.

plunder To take without right; to steal.

producer A recording engineer who also helps groups work on their ideas in the studio.

set A live musical performance by a band in front of an audience.

105

single A song released by itself, usually accompanied by one other song for the second side of the record.

sitar Indian string instrument with a long neck like a guitar.

skiffle A blend of country and rock and roll music that was very popular in Britain in the late 1950s.

string quartet Four musicians all playing classical stringed instruments.

studio A place where music is recorded.

swagger To walk with an air of self-confidence.

tape loop A piece of audiotape pieced together to form a loop. The loop has sounds recorded on it, so when played back, it replays the sound repetitively.

venue A place where performances are held.

vinyl Slang word for a traditional record album, which is made from polyvinyl chloride. Most albums sold today are compact discs.

TO FIND OUT MORE

Rock and Roll Hall of Fame and Museum
One Key Plaza
Cleveland, OH 44114
(888) 764-ROCK (7625)
Web site: http://www.rockhall.com

Web Sites

BeatleBrunch.com
http://www.beatlebrunch.com

TheBeatles.com
http://www.thebeatles.com

The Beatles Discography
http://hollywoodandvine.com/beatles

The Internet Beatles Album
http://www.getback.org

Martin, Marvin. *The Beatles: The Music Was Never the Same.* Danbury, CT: Franklin Watts, Inc., 1996.

Venezia, Mike. *The Beatles.* Danbury, CT: Children's Press, 1997.

Woog, Adam. *The Beatles.* San Diego: Lucent Books, 1997.

Wright, David K. *John Lennon: The Beatles and Beyond.* Berkeley Heights, NJ: Enslow Publishers, Inc., 1996.

Works Cited

Davies, Hunter. *The Beatles.* New York: W.W. Norton & Company, Inc., 1996.

Martin, George. *With a Little Help from My Friends: The Making of Sgt. Pepper.* New York: Little, Brown & Company, 1995.

McCartney, Paul, George Harrison, Ringo Starr, and John Lennon. *The Beatles Anthology.* San Francisco: Chronicle Books, 2000.

INDEX

CREDITS

About the Author

Jim Wentzel has worked in the Web industry for the past six years. He loves his wife, his two-year-old son, his guitars, and making music of all kinds. He can also be found singing in his car, listening to music while driving to work on most days.

Photo Credits

Cover © Underwood & Underwood/Corbis; pp. 4, 6, 18, 48, 68, 95 © Bettmann/Corbis; pp. 5, 17, 28, 36, 39, 41, 50, 58, 64, 70, 76, 84, 88 © Michael Ochs Archive; pp. 8, 11, 14, 21, 22, 31, 32, 33, 34, 43, 45, 47, 54–55, 67, 73, 79, 81, 90 © Hulton Archive by Getty Images; p. 52 © AP/Wide World Photos; p. 92 © Henry Diltz/Corbis; p. 97 © AFP/Corbis; p. 100 © Hilton-Deutsch Collection/Corbis.

Layout and Design

Thomas Forget